THE SIMPLE TRUTH ABOUT MONEY

Unless otherwise indicated, scripture quotations
are taken from the Holy Bible,
King James Version (KJV)

www.change-ministry.org
change_ministry@yahoo.com

ISBN   978-1-300-77970-4

THE

SIMPLE

TRUTH

ABOUT

MONEY

Felisha D. McRae

Table of Contents

This book is dedicated to those that are struggling in their finances and feel that there is no hope. I am prayerful that you will become enlighten and encouraged to know that there is nothing too hard for God and your life is not beyond repair.

Making life changing solutions to our everyday living that will lead to life patterns reversing for our good, is my desire for you as you walk through these pages with me.

Changing habits is a life journey so this book was not intended to show you how to get money but how to handle the money that God has already given you and even gain increase with following a discipline life style, having principals, making right choices and finally own it.

So as you go on this journey with me I pray the blessings of the Lord upon you and great success.

This book was birth out of a teaching at New Destiny Ministry. I am thankful for the opportunity that was given to me to teach on such a sensitive subject.

Out of this teaching birth a new level of success and confidence. It inspired hope that whatever your dilemma, you can make it and you can be free from debt and the bondages and chains of failure that at times hold us all captive at every level of life we are living.

I am prayerful that this book will bring a quick turnaround in lives of the readers and that each of you know you are Winners, more than conquerors in Christ Jesus.

I am grateful to God for the wisdom and insight that He has given me to share with you on the simple facts about money.

I don't claim to have all the answers and it is so much I don't know, but I am hopeful that this I am sharing will bless you and enlighten you. My desire is, as you read this booklet it will give you better insight to some of the situations you may be facing or have faced. A lot of time when we talk about money we can become defensive, intimidating or rebellious.

Money is such a sensitive subject that has to be handled with tenderness and open mindedness. I always say the greatest sin is not in the fall but in the staying down in the fall. Okay. I have fallen now how can I get back up. Sometimes we tend to waller in the mess of our mistakes too long. I am prayerful that you will be encouraged as you read this book and inspired to do great things concerning your finances.

I hope that as you read you will find where you stand and how you can improve and go to a higher place. During this economic crisis that our nation face, we find that we all have been in circumstances that we would not think we would ever face. We all have seasons and times of good days and bad days. We have times that we are the giver and then there are times we have to be on the receiving end.

We have to be careful that when hard times come, pride does not come with it. We all at times have to face difficult times of one thing or another, but it's how we handle it that will determine our outcome. During these times we have to pull from many resources until we find what works for us.

Rebuilding for what ever situation, whether it was your fault or not or whether this dilemma that you bear is beyond your control, rebuilding can be hard. With dedication, commitment and faithfulness to your budget it can be done. I encourage you today to focus on a fresh start, regroup and train your mind that you are a winner and you will regain your loss and be greater than your former success.

There are many books on success out there on how to gain wealth. We can read all the books in the world but until we take ownership of our life and what we expect to gain from life, no book in the world will help.

We have to first recognize that there is a problem and that I need help. I always say that when you are sick you must first identify that you are sick and then make a conscience decision to go the doctor, and then follow the directions that he gives you. So as it is with our finances *"Own It"* the problem, then take the necessary steps to work your way out. Tell yourself I don't like this place I am in, Now talk to yourself that this is temporary, and I won't always be in this condition, and then see yourself coming out of it.

Position yourself, elevate your mind and separate yourself from that which would cause you to fail and now work the plan. You are a winner and you can do this.

Change "aint" Change until I Change
"Things will Change" because I "Change"

Things that will keep us out of trouble.......

1. The number one cause to a bad relationship, whether it is a friendship, marital, or business relationship is the *Lack of Money, or the Mismanagement of Money.*

2. Spending more than what you make or what you have is a problem.

3. Spending based on what you are expecting to come is a problem...... example income taxed or a pay check.

4. Avoid Folks that borrow and forget to pay back, or just don't pay back money, make an argument to keep from paying back money owed.

5. Avoid folk with bad creditability ... that's why their credit is bad because they don't like to pay back.

6. Focus on having good name it will take you further than money , riches and gold.

7. Don't let Money control you.....You take control of Money.

The Real Truth About Money

8. Don't be an impulsive spender. Make conscience decisions you are spending your money on.

9. If you have money and good credit... Avoid people who never have money and don't care about having good credit...

10. Never let people control your money or business who cannot control their money or business,

If they can't manage their money how then will they be able to manage yours

11. Know What , When, Where Your money is going ... Give an account for your spending

12. Don't always be available to lend a helping hand especially to the same person who is in trouble continuously.

When loaning Money, be watchful how it is paid back, whether it is paid back the way it was promised, to determine whether you will loan to that person again. For example: often times we expect our money back all at once then it's return back in small increments, or not at the expected time.

Know how you are going to pay back your debt before you borrow money...Then stick to the plan...Sometimes we never pay back the borrowed money, before we need more money, after spending that money we need to borrow again and we become deeper in debt to our debtors. It is a bad thing to have multiple loans when your money is so limited.

Everyone has had a financial crisis at some point in their lives, but you must get to the root of your problem.   Look up and see yourself going forth. Don't allow yourself to get stuck in the ruts and sink lower no matter how bad it may look.   There is hope but it's also take, discipline, and hard work to recover your money, your credit, and your life back.

If You Follow This Simple Plan And Work It....It Will Work For You And You Will Find Yourself Back On Your Feet.

You Must First Have A Desire To Change Your Situation, Then Change Your Thinking, The Way You Talk, And Who You Associate With. Poverty Begets Poverty! Avoid People That Don't Want Anything And Is Not Doing Anything With Their Life. They Will Only Drain Your Strength And Even Your Resources

Money And Power Attracts Each Other And At Times It Can Be Intimidating To Those Who Have No Desire To Prosper Or Change their Lifestyle.

Don't Be Offended Concerning Your Situation. Become Enlighten.   Pursue Someone Who Has A Strong Grip On Budgeting Money and Allow Someone to Help You And Become Focus And Educated.

The word of God declares if you are faithful over little I will make you ruler over much. Stir your-self, wake yourself.   If you sleep too long you may miss the many blessings that the Lord has for you. The blessings of the Lord will make you rich if you will work what He has already given you. He has given us all something to work with.   We just have to tap in and use it.   Many people have come out of debt by using their God given talent right from their home.

Realize What You Have Been Doing Is Not Working For You — Change Your Mind And Your Plan.

No Drive- No Passion- No Work = No Results

You May Need A Different Approach And A New Strategy. Find A Plan That Fit You Personally So You Will Succeed.   You Need A No — Fail Plan.

A Personal Design For Your Situation Something That You Know That You Can Live With.

Work On Establishing A Good Name, and Good Credit Again, Even If You Start Small. You Got To Started Somewhere.

Never Pay Back Money With A Hope Plan, But With A Sure Plan....

Hope Plan Is "I Am Hoping I Get This Money On Friday".

Sure Plan Is I" Know That I Am Getting This Money On Friday".

Know How You Are Going To Pay Back Your Debt Before You Borrow It, Then Stick To The Plan.....

Be Careful Loaning Money. A Lot Of Times When People Get Money They Get Funny Or Disappear. When loaning out money on a personal level know that person character and credibility. If you can not afford to loan out money "Don't Do It". It is always a chance you may never see your money again and ruin a good relationship.

Don't Run With People Who Are In The Same State You Are In: Broke Folk Can Not Help You Come Up In Life. Only Thing You Can Do For Each Other Is Exchange You Misery.

Work On A Plan And Stay Focus: A Lazy Man Without A Plan Will Never Win

Become Responsible For Your Action And Accountable. Take Charge Of You And Your Money.

Learn How To Manage Money Or You Will Always Be In A Bad Place.

Your money needs may seem like a Permanent Condition but we always give it a temporal fix…. Money
Will Come And Money Will Go. Getting money is
not the problem, keeping money seems to be the
problem… you need to find a permanent answer
instead of a temporal solution. You have to become
tired of the way you have been living and do something about it.

We Perish Because The Lack Of Knowledge Not
From The Lack Of Money …… God Shows Us How
To Get Money, But We Need Wisdom On How To
Keep Money And Make It Work For Us….. He Gives
Us Power To Get Wealth.

The Word Says I Wish Above All… "Everything"
That You Prosper. God Wants Us To Prosper.

The Blessings Of The Lord Make Rich And It Add
No Sorrow. It is Us That Cause The Sorrow By
Walking In Error. How Many Of You Want To
"Change" Your Financial State.

There Is A Difference In Changing And Fixing.....
Change Is Permanent- A New Way Of Thinking

Fixing Is Temporal -A Just A Quick Fix

You Got to Become Tired Of Your State And Get Mad, Then Tell Yourself Enough Is Enough. The word of God declares you have dwell here long enough

Faith Without Works Is Dead- So Let's Get Busy And Begin To Grind

Shake Yourself, Wake Up Tell Yourself I've Been Napping Long Enough

Have A Vision For Success And See Yourself Out Of The Rut

Tell Yourself......
"I Can" "I Will" "I Shall"

Throw Out....
I Can't, I Ain't, I Won't, And I Don't Know

Write Your Vision And Run With

(Read) *Job 36:11   Eccl 11:1,   Eccl 11: 4-6*

From My House To God's House I Pray Debt Cancellation, I Pray Increase, I Pray Overflow... That God Will Bless Your Going Out And Coming In.... And Everything That Pertain To You, Everything That You Touch, Everywhere You Go. That He Will Attach You With Greatness And You Will Fulfilled Destiny And Purpose. That The Lord Has Already Spoke Concerning You And The Promise That Await You.

Here Is A Simple Questionnaire That May Help You Get Back On Track

Working Through Your Money Struggle

1. What Is Your Biggest Financial Concern?

2. Do You Have A Money Strategy?

3. What Are Your Plans For The Future?

4. Make A Plan To Save A Minimum Of $5.00 Per Week For A Year.

5. Are You Willing To Make The Necessary Sacrifices It Take To Become Debt Free Or Comfortable With Your Finances?

6. Do You Wish To Become More Knowledgeable In Becoming More Financially Stable?

7. Do You Have A Budget?

8. Are You Faithful In Following Your Budget?

9. Do You Know How To Prepare And Follow A Budget?

10. Do You Spend Out More Money Than You Make Or Have?

11. Do You Really Need The Things That You Buy?

12. Do You Have A Savings?

13. Do You Take Out More Often Than You Put Into Your Savings?

14. How Can You Cut Back In Your Lifestyle And What Can You Let Go?

15. Which Do You Do More; Pay On Your Bills Or Pay Your Bills?

16. Do You Keep Bills Longer Than You Really Need Instead Of Paying Them Off?

17. Do You Have A Lot Of Little Nagging Unnecessary Bills That You Should Get Rid Of?

18. Do You Spend As Soon As Money Comes Into Your Hands?

19. Can You Whole On To Money Longer Than A Month And Think Long Before Spending?

20. Do You Plan Spending Or Shop By Impulse?

21. Do You Shop Around For Bargains And Wait For Sales?

22. Do You Set Financial Goals?

23. How Well Is Your Credit?

24. How Long Will It Take To Repair? And Will You Repair It?

25. If You Lose Your Job How Will You Survive?

26. Are You A Paycheck From Homeless?

27. Be Honest How Discipline Is You With Money?

28. How Well Can You Handle Money?

29. Do You Feel Like You Are Focus, Have Direction, Or Is Out Of Control When It Comes To You Finances?

30. Would You Like Help With Your Finances To Get Better Control?

31. How Often Do You Try To Pay Your Debts Off Early?

32. Are You Always Late Paying Your Bills?

33. Should God Trust You With His Money? And If He Gives You Debt Freedom Could He Trust You To Be A Good Steward?

Felisha D McRae
Change Ministry, Inc.

Examine Yourself

Take this time to answer a few questions and make a few notes that you feel that will help you accomplish the goals you would like to meet for this year.

1. After you have finished this book take time to digest and examine what you would like to do.

2. What are some of the dumbest choices you ever made concerning handling your money?

3. How can you become debt free and stay free of debt?

4. What are your greatest struggles you have as it pertain to money?

The simple truths about money and the lack of it........

Discipline

Commitment

Honesty

Owning Up

Faithfulness

Being Responsible

Identifying

Open Minded

Excepting Help

These are a few principles that will help you achieve your goals in turning your finances around.

Best Wishes

This book is a celebration to myself and of the things the Lord is doing in my life. Often times, we celebrate others and don't take the time to celebrate what the Lord is doing in our own lives.

We can become too occupied with those around us and lose focus of our own destiny and accomplishments. It is good to be a blessing to others, but you have to know the investment that the Lord has in you. If you can't see it how do you think others will be able to identify what the Lord is doing in you. You got to know where the Lord is taking you in order to give anybody a road map to your life, so if you don't know where you are going and who you are, you can't expect others to have the vision for you and your journey.

In this next season of your life celebrate you and give God the Glory for what he is doing, his marvelous works at hand. For all the people who has wondered or thought where is Prophetess McRae, what happen to Change Ministry, where are they now and what is she doing......*"For after you have suffered awhile He will settle you, establish you, and perfect you."*

Thank You

I am back walking in my Now. I have been on the other side of the mountain, I have been in hiding. Walking with a General, a time of grooming, a time of perfecting and fine tuning for the next level of anointing that is coming my way, for the next position that I will step into and for the next place of uncommon ground the Lord will take me.

Cast down, but not destroy....Persecuted, but not forsaken..... Yes, I was injured but not killed in the battle for the Lord hid me in his tabernacle, he hid me in a secret place where the enemy could not find me.....

I count it a great pleasure and an honor to have been placed in the care of such a great General as Pastor Dr. Geraldine Eady for such a time to watch over my soul, to nurture and protect what God has invested in me through her guidance.

Money cannot pay, nor words express my gratitude for regaining life to live again. I can truly say what a pioneer to follow, what a general to lead, Because of being in the right place, at the right time, with the right instructions *I live, I am restored, I am revived.*

I am Thankful for your faithfulness to God's tutorial training Ground. When I say I couldn't—I did... having done all to stand even though I at times I lean.

I am still standing in spite of it all. I can truly say there is an after and in the end we do Win.

Change Ministry and Prophetess McRae is back and thriving.

Thank you Pastor Eady for accepting the assignment of pulling me out of a horrible pit. A great reward will be charge to your account.....

Here is a great tool to help save money for every week that you are in you save that amount for example the first week you save one dollar the ten week you save ten dollars the fifty second week you save fifty two dollars by the end of the year you would have save 1,378 isn't that great and easy to do

52 Week Money Challenge

WEEK	DEPOSIT AMOUNT	ACCOUNT BALANCE		WEEK	DEPOSIT AMOUNT	ACCOUNT BALANCE
1	$1.00	$1.00		27	$27.00	$378.00
2	$2.00	$3.00		28	$28.00	$406.00
3	$3.00	$6.00		29	$29.00	$435.00
4	$4.00	$10.00		30	$30.00	$465.00
5	$5.00	$15.00		31	$31.00	$496.00
6	$6.00	$21.00		32	$32.00	$528.00
7	$7.00	$28.00		33	$33.00	$561.00
8	$8.00	$36.00		34	$34.00	$595.00
9	$9.00	$45.00		35	$35.00	$630.00
10	$10.00	$55.00		36	$36.00	$666.00
11	$11.00	$66.00		37	$37.00	$703.00
12	$12.00	$78.00		38	$38.00	$741.00
13	$13.00	$91.00		39	$39.00	$780.00
14	$14.00	$105.00		40	$40.00	$820.00
15	$15.00	$120.00		41	$41.00	$861.00
16	$16.00	$136.00		42	$42.00	$903.00
17	$17.00	$153.00		43	$43.00	$946.00
18	$18.00	$171.00		44	$44.00	$990.00
19	$19.00	$190.00		45	$45.00	$1,035.00
20	$20.00	$210.00		46	$46.00	$1,081.00
21	$21.00	$231.00		47	$47.00	$1,128.00
22	$22.00	$253.00		48	$48.00	$1,176.00
23	$23.00	$276.00		49	$49.00	$1,125.00
24	$24.00	$300.00		50	$50.00	$1,275.00
25	$25.00	$325.00		51	$51.00	$1,326.00
26	$26.00	$351.00		52	$52.00	$1,378.00

Personal Notes

Personal Notes

Personal Notes

About the Author

Prophetess Felisha D. McRae, reared and educated in the Public School System in Glynn County, Georgia and is a student at Destiny Bible College pursuing a Bachelor's Degree in Christian Education.

Prophetess McRae is the founder and overseer of Change Ministry, Inc; which she birthed out of a home ministry in 2006. The ministry traveled from home to home in the surrounding areas; then expanded to the jails, nursing homes and rehabilitation centers. Then God led her to bring the ministry out of the field into a church setting where she pastored a small group to people for a while.

In 2007, she formed a prayer group, "Warriors on the move for Jesus" which brought women together from all walks of life supporting each other and those in need.

She is the author of the book "I Survived the Storm"; which is an insight into her own life story. The book was published in 2008, and has been read across many continents.

Her mission is to teach women the biblical principles of faith, love, healing, prosperity, redemption, righteousness and hope; using a non-traditional approach. These teachings allow women to discuss concerns and issues, therefore, bringing emotional and spiritual healing to all areas of their lives.

God has birthed out of Prophetess McRae an anointing to minister to women in an unusual way. She promotes and conducts workshops and conferences throughout the United States. She travels extensively conducting revivals, which brings a renewal and a refreshing to all.

Prophetess McRae is the mother of two children, *Percy II* and *'Kristian-Nichole'*, and is the founder of **Change Women**, an open forum mentorship program for women. She serves as the Associate Pastor of New Destiny Evangelistic Ministry.

Her motto is: *"On a common ground, operating in an uncommon anointing, which brings about an explosive deliverance. "*

I am available for...

Therapeutic Groups

Workshops

Conferences

Women's Fellowship

Revivals

• •

If you would like Change Women's Ministry to come......

Visit

Pray

Speak To You

Contact:
Felisha D. McRae
Post Office Box 2635
Brunswick, Ga. 31521
912-223-1847

Visit my website for more information and to purchase other books

www.change-ministry.org

www.ingramcontent.com/pod-product-compliance
Lightning Source LLC
Chambersburg PA
CBHW021857170526
45157CB00006B/2490